JOE BURROW

HOW JOE BURROW BECAME THE NFL'S TOP YOUNG QUARTERBACK

By

JACKSON CARTER

Copyright © 2020

TABLE OF CONTENTS

LEGAL NOTES

Joe Burrow is meant for entertainment and educational use only. All attempts have been made to present factual information in an unbiased context.

BORN TO WIN

With media and Hollywood so caught up in the big cities, it can be hard for many people to picture the life of a small-town person without thinking of the way that sort of life has been portrayed on the screen. However, the small American towns are still very much alive and present today, and many of those we see on the internet or TV hail from those out-of-nowhere locales. Some of the best athletes got their start in small towns, only to end up playing in arenas and stadiums that could hold more people in the stands than they'd even grown up around in their hometown. However, by the time most people get out of that small-town lifestyle and spend some time in the spotlight, they decide that when all is said and done, they prefer the hustle and bustle of the larger cities to where they grew up. A small group, however, makes it a point to not just go back to their hometowns but to also give back to them once they get the opportunity to. One up and coming NFL star is one of those people who has vowed to head back to his hometown, and during the COVID-19 pandemic, he did just that, even moving back into his childhood Star Wars-themed bedroom in his parent's home. It seemed that moving through college football and into the NFL wasn't enough to take that small-town vibe away from him.

Joseph Lee Burrows was born on December 10, 1996. His father, Jim Burrow, and mother, Robin Burrow, welcomed their third son into the family. Joe's two older brothers, Jamie and Dan, were from Jim's previous marriage, but the boys, Jim and Robin, were a close-knit group, adding another generation to a long line of athletes and sports-minded people. Living in Ames, Iowa, Joe's father, Jim, worked as part of the coaching staff for the Iowa State Cyclones. He had been a great athlete himself, back before starting a family. He had played football for Ole Miss before eventually transferring to Nebraska. Later, he ended up being drafted by the Green Bay Packers in the 1976 NFL Draft. An eighth-round pick, he only ended up playing in three games as a cornerback for the Packers, but this gave him the resume that transferred into a successful stint in the Canadian Football League. There, he played for the Montreal Alouettes as well as the Calgary Stampeders and Ottawa Rough Riders. With the Alouettes, Jim was part of the team when they made three Grey Cup finals appearances and eventually went on to win the championship as well. He even ended up making the CFL Eastern Conference All-Star Team in back-to-back seasons in both 1978 and '79. After leaving as a player and starting a family, Jim transitioned his talent and skills to coaching instead of playing.

However, this wasn't the only source of athleticism that was running through Joe's blood. In fact, way back in 1940, Jim's grandmother was a talented basketball player in high school. According to the records, she set a Mississippi state high school record of points scored in a single game. She scored 82 points! Additionally, Joe's paternal grandfather had also played basketball at Mississippi State. His uncle, John, also played football, but this time at Ole Miss during his college years. Joe's two older brothers were also talented athletes and they ended up playing at their dad's alma mater, the University of Nebraska, when it was time for them to head off to college. Needless to say, Joe was constantly surrounded by athletes and exposed to sports from a young age. In fact, that could have been one of the contributing factors that led Joe to follow the path that he did with so many different football-minded men around him throughout his childhood.

When he was just five, he got to see his father and his older brother working together at the same time as Jamie played as the starting middle linebacker at Nebraska while Jim was the assistant coach there. They played in the 2001 Rose Bowl and Joe was able to have a much more personal connection to the event. With his older brothers so much bigger and older than him, it was clear that growing up, Joe always faced faster, stronger opponents in his brothers, which, his father said, affected Joe's style of play given that he is much more physical than many of the others his age.

Soon after witnessing his dad and brother at the Rose Bowl, Joe began to play in the local youth football leagues. However, although he came from a long line of football players, even at the beginning of his football career, he was putting his own spin on things. Unlike his father, uncle, and older brothers, Joe didn't line up on the defensive side of the ball. He started as the quarterback instead, something that happened by chance as the first team he played for didn't have anyone else that could play the position, so it went to Joe without contest. Already at that young age, with his family ties to the college football scene, Joe set himself a goal to achieve in the future: to win a college championship one day.

A few years later, when Jim was hired as the defensive coordinator at North Dakota State, the family moved to Fargo, North Dakota. Joe would get the chance on some occasions to visit his dad at work, sitting in the college coaching offices when he was just seven years old. On one of those occasions, Dan Enos, the man that would eventually coach Central Michigan took note of the young boy visiting his dad. He turned to Jim and told him that Joe had a future in football, fueling Joe's young dreams even more.

The Burrow family spent the next couple of years in North Dakota and Joe continued to play and develop as a player. However, he wasn't solely dedicated to football as he was a natural athlete and tried his hand at a number of sports, spending a lot of time playing football, basketball, and baseball as well. Then Jim had to move again and the family was forced to move. This time, Jim had accepted a position as the defensive coordinator at Ohio University and the family followed him to Athens, Ohio, where they would be staying. There, Joe began to really develop as he grew and moved into his high school years.

THE START OF THE LEGEND

After moving from different schools and states multiple times while growing up, the family felt at home living in Ohio and Joe became a much more confident and comfortable part of the school and community. With his dad working for Ohio University, Joe had the opportunity to make friends, stick with them for more than just a few years, and eventually go to high school with them as well. In 2011, he became a freshman at Athens High School in The Plains, Ohio, a tiny community of about 20,000 people. There, Joe truly began to blossom into a young man, and not just as a star athlete.

His former high school teacher remembers back to what Joe was like during his high school years and recalls a smart and kind young man. Of course, there was always going to be the shadow of football and sports surrounding him because he was such a natural talent, but for this teacher, he remembered who he was as a person as well. For example, he stated that Joe was very intelligent, had an excellent memory, and was regularly one of the smartest students in the class, a class of eccentric but interesting students who seemed to bypass clique lines and made sure that they took care of each other. Another memory is of Joe reaching out to those who were isolated. As a new kid at a school more than once, it was probably easy for Joe to spot those who stood out from the crowd. Those with disabilities, those who were left as loners, Joe's teacher said;

those are the ones that Joe would specifically reach out to and talk with, even choosing them for his basketball team during PE just to make them feel more connected. This trait is something that, he said, truly marked him as a leader amongst his peers and not just on the field or the court.

During his middle school, Joe spent a lot of time in sports, splitting his time and the seasons between football, basketball, and baseball respectively. While he had a lot of fun playing football, his main passions were basketball and baseball. But everything changed when he entered high school. With a new coach and a new system to get used to, Joe found himself becoming more and more dedicated and in love with football as his main pursuit. Still, he continued to play the other sports and played them well. As a basketball player, he averaged 17.1 points and 6.9 rebounds in the three years that he played for the team in high school. However, over time, slowly but surely, he developed more interest in football and spent more and more of his time and effort bringing out the best in himself in football than the other sports.

His coaches saw this and were happy to have him continue to play a bigger role in their team's designs. According to one of his former coaches, it was Nathan White who had really opened Joe's eyes to the possibilities of football and the spread offense really clicked with Joe's own style and goals as a quarterback. Joe, his coaches said, was extremely creative and simply loved the game and loved to find himself in different situations that he'd never been in because he had a natural knack for sorting them out and doing really well. As a team, they knew they could count on him to do what needed to be done regardless of what they asked of him and where they put him on the field. In fact, White even told Joe, as a freshman, that White believed that Joe had what it took to play at Ohio State; that he was that good of a player and he'd only been there for one season at that point. Still, this confidence and support from the coaching staff really helped Joe figure out his game and his own confidence levels. And although he was the young guy on the team, he stepped into leadership roles early on.

By the time he was a sophomore, Joe was putting up big numbers and showing up as a real force for the team. He had over 200 completions that season, as well as 3,239 passing yards during his second year of high school. He had a 62.2 percent completion rate for passing, which went up the next two years. As a 15-year old kid, he also threw for 47 touchdowns as well as rushing for 836 yards. For such a young player, it was clear that he had the talent to burn, and everyone was excited to see what the next two years would bring, especially now that he was beginning to hit his growth spurt years.

According to his former teammates and coaches, it wasn't just the natural talent and growth, though that helped Joe over the course of the next few years. He was extremely confident in himself, they said, and he led by example, never expecting anything that he himself wouldn't do, which included the hard work between games and during the off-season. They all remember Joe as the guy who would consistently show up on a daily basis and put in the work, doing it with a positive attitude and chasing his dreams. He consistently showed get better each day than he had been the previous day, inspiring those around him to do their best as well. As a leader and star of the team, that went a long way to encourage the rest of his teammates to continue to show up and work on their own games. The natural talents he had, though, continued to grow as he put in the time and work over those next seasons. And it clearly showed.

During his junior year, he had another 200 plus completions throughout the season, going from 3,239 yards to 3,732. He added on to that by bumping up his completion rate from 62.2 percent to 71.2, jumping up almost a full ten percent more than he had completed during his sophomore season. He matched his sophomore season with 47 touchdowns as a junior and again put up over 575 yards rushing that third year. Needless to say, he was drawing a lot of attention from colleges already and they were all watching as he continued to get better and better as each game passed.

Then, just when it looked as though he had set himself up nicely as a quarterback stud, the team needed something more from him. When facing Tri-Valley during the second round of the playoffs, the undefeated Athens team needed to shake things up to handle the single-wing offense and running game that Tri-Valley brought. In the middle of the game, the coaches made a decision to put their star quarterback on defense, pushing him to play both sides of the ball for the remainder of the game in the hopes that he could help make a difference.

Although he'd played a quarterback his whole life, playing defense came naturally to him. As the son of a coach, especially a defensive coordinator, it was clear from the first snap that although Joe had grown up on the offensive side of things, his skill of breaking down the game, thanks to his dad and older brothers, served him well and he took to the position well. In fact, it was clear to everyone that although he was always needed to play quarterback because he was great at it, he wouldn't have had any difficulty playing cornerback full time, or even safety if his arm hadn't ended up working out; he was that naturally athletic and had such a broad knowledge of the game that he could do well in many different positions. During that game against Tri-Valley, he didn't just help lead the team on offense, he was also able to make a couple of really key plays on defense as well, one of them being an interception late in the game to help them seal their 41-20 win as they advanced through the playoffs.

That wasn't the last time, however, that everyone would get to watch their star quarterback play defense. In fact, when the starting cornerback eventually quit the team, they needed Joe there more often. As the playoffs progressed and the Athens went on to the state championship game playing against Toledo Central Catholic, they called upon him once more. Toledo had a poor passing game, but had a number of Division I running backs, so they put Joe out there again and watched him work his arm, then his legs.

It is not very often that a quarterback is required to make a tackle in a game, but it does happen. When this happens, it is usually with clenched teeth that the coaching staff watches on as they make sure that the quarterback tackles that player but does it without injuring himself. After all, the quarterback is the lynchpin of the offense and the team, and without him, it would be really difficult to score points or lead the way to victory. As a result, many quarterbacks, despite having the raw speed and talent for playing a position like cornerback or safety, never really see themselves in that position because they're needed as a quarterback more. However, thanks to growing up with a football family and two older brothers, Joe was more than ready to take on the opposing offense's running backs, tackling and taking them down as needed, and doing it well and without injuring himself.

As a multi-faceted player, he was able to take advantage of the agility that he had as a quarterback, dancing around in the pocket to get off the blocks early as a cornerback, and his confidence and lack of fear of injury, thanks to his experience, helped him become an aggressive and efficient defensive player. He was, his coach even recalls, one of the two best tacklers on the team; he just hadn't had a chance to show it because he'd been stuck at quarterback up until then. Plus, paired with his football IQ, coaches were confident that he knew just as well as they did, what was needed from him, and how he could accomplish it, making it a great fit for him to show off even more of his natural athleticism and capabilities and removing any doubt anyone might have about him playing at the next level in college.

Senior Year

In his senior year, things continued to get better and better. That year, he threw for 4,445 yards, a staggering 700-yard improvement on his junior season. He also bumped up his completion rating to 72.3 percent and threw a new high of 63 touchdowns in his senior year. He continued to rush as well, putting up over 575 yards again. And he achieved all this in only fifteen games of the season. Throughout that season, his 63 touchdowns were only countered by two interceptions for the whole season. He'd grown to a six-foot-three-inch, 215-pound senior and was ready to play both offense and defense whenever required by his team.

Over the course of his high school career, Joe had a terrific showing. Not only did he fill the quarterback position to the point that he led his team to multiple victories, playoff wins, and even a championship, but he also helped the team by filling in on defense and laying down some big hits and plays on that side of the ball. Throughout his football career at Athens, he threw for a total of 11,416 yards and rushed for another 2,067. He had a tremendous 157 total touchdowns from passing and 27 rushing in the three years (sophomore to senior year) that he was the starting quarterback. Although he had been raised in a football family that was dominated by defensive players, he ended up becoming, some said, one of the best quarterbacks to come out of Ohio schools since 1982 when Art Schlichter who was at Ohio

State was drafted as the number four overall pick in the draft that year.

Joe had led the team to the playoffs all three years he started and also led them to their first seven playoff wins ever. He was recognized as a talented quarterback and an all-around threat on the field. He ended up winning a few awards in his senior year. Ohio named him the Mr. Football Award winner and he was also the Gatorade Player of the Year for his final year at Athens in 2014. That year, he'd helped lead the team to a terrific 14-1 record, but that wasn't all. He continued to play basketball as a point guard and was even named to the first-team all-state team in his senior year. Obviously, he became known and recognized in the community as a stellar athlete. In fact, he left such a great impression on the school and community that in December of 2019, the local school district's school board decided that they needed to do something to honor him. They voted unanimously to rename the high school football stadium in his name.

By the end of his football career in high school, he was ranked as a four-star recruit and colleges began to knock on his door to get a chance to see him in their school's uniform. Additionally, as a dual-threat quarterback, he was seen as the eighth-highest in his class. He received a number of offers from schools like Iowa State, Central Michigan, North Carolina State, and more. However, in the end, he ended up with an offer from Ohio State, his dream school. He decided to go ahead and take that offer, committing to Ohio State in May of his senior year.

THE OHIO STATE CALLS

So after graduation from Athens, Joe packed up and moved away from his home. However, he didn't move too far. In fact, the Ohio State Columbus campus was just 75 miles northwest of where he had been living with his family for the past few years. This meant that he didn't have to drive too far when he wanted to come back home, and, in fact, it was rumored that his mom would even drive the 75 miles there and back to do his laundry for him, a fact that he sheepishly admitted to. This allowed him a bit of freedom and independence but didn't completely remove him from the tight-knit family and community that he'd been a part of.

In his first year at Ohio State, he redshirted, allowing him the chance to get used to the new college life and the college level of play. Coming from a small town in the middle of nowhere, Ohio meant that moving up to college level was a huge adjustment due to the sheer volume of talent that he'd now be up against. Over the course of that year and the following two years, he was relegated to a backup position to the team's current quarterback, J. T. Barrett. During his sophomore and junior seasons, Joe only racked up ten appearances for the team, only throwing a total of 29 for 39. This meant that over those three years with the Ohio State team, he had only 287 yards to his name and just two touchdowns, a staggering difference compared to the opportunities and playtime he had in high school.

Despite this lackluster career for the football team, Joe found other things to occupy his time. Instead, he turned to his studies. He majored in Consumer and Family Financial Services and worked hard to take as many classes as he could while also juggling practices and games. Because of this dedication to his studies, Joe was actually able to graduate and finish his degree in just three years. This worked out perfectly, actually, because he saw that his place on the football team wasn't what he was hoping it would be and he needed to make some changes. When the team brought in Dwayne Haskins, another quarterback, Joe understood that Haskins would end up taking over the lead position after Barrett's move into the NFL during Joe's senior season. As a result, he began to look for other options.

Having earned his degree and officially graduating, he was now eligible to transfer to different schools as a graduate, something that allowed him a bit more freedom in selecting a school that he felt would work best for him. As he shopped around for different programs, two came to the forefront: Cincinnati and Louisiana State University. As decision time got closer and closer, it was clear that Joe was really leaning toward Cincinnati, but he still had an opportunity to visit both schools before making a commitment to either one. He had personally asked each team to meet with them and he, as well as his family, went on a trip together to see the schools and meet the coaches and staff there.

On the first day of the trip, the Burrows visited Cincinnati. Those following his decision seemed to believe that he had a strong opinion of the school and its team and that he was really favoring them in the process. However, Ed Orgeron, the LSU coach, was in his second season with the school and was anxious to show Joe everything the school had to offer, as well as what he'd be getting by moving to somewhere as culturally rich as Louisiana.

When Joe, his dad, and brother, Dan, arrived in Louisiana, they were greeted by the coach and his staff and saw that Joe wasn't interested in the typical recruitment process. Instead, Joe was focused primarily on football. As a graduate, he'd already experienced the schooling side and had finished his degree, but he still had two years of eligibility and wouldn't have to sit for a year due to the transfer, so he wanted to make sure that he picked a school that would get him in there and would be a program that he'd be able to work well with for his short time there. Orgeron and his staff could see this and they took the family out to a fancy restaurant the first night of the visit, but quickly followed it up with a three-hour meeting at the school going over a film. They had put together a film of not only Joe's time playing at Ohio State, but they also compared his skills and options in those clips to the plays that they ran at LSU.

With this, the coaches were able to share with Joe their plan for him in their team and really show him what it would be like to play as an LSU Tiger. Not only that, but they were able to ask him what he saw, his reads, and his thoughts on the way plays unfolded from their previous quarterback clips. This gave them a chance as well to see what kind of player he was, what he thought about the game, and how great his football presence and IQ were. They liked what they saw and felt like Joe was also impressed by what they had shown him regarding his possible future at LSU. Following the long lunch meeting, the Burrow family joined the coaches for dinner at a local seafood restaurant and it seemed that Joe had really taken a liking to the local food, especially the boiled crawfish.

On May 20, 2018, Joe made his decision and chose his future school as Louisiana State University, officially becoming a Tiger when he moved to Baton Rouge and began working with the team. His former teammate, J. T. Barrett, was excited about Joe's new opportunity. He stated that he was aware that Joe had been hoping for more time at Ohio State but that didn't stop Joe from being a standout person and good sport. He had brought a great attitude and a sense of determination and hard work to the team, acknowledging the fact that he wasn't going to be the one getting many of the snaps. However, Barrett was sure that at LSU, Joe would be getting a great chance to showcase his talent and he knew that all Joe needed was a chance and he was going to do great things when he finally got it.

Down On the Bayou

Obviously moving to Baton Rouge was a huge change for Joe, who had spent the previous three years just over an hour away from his family and hometown. Now, he'd be forced to make a fresh start in a new state much further away from the comforts and familiarity of Ohio, not to mention he'd have to do his own laundry. For Joe, he shared that the change was hard at first, especially getting used to the new culture he found himself in. As a health nut, he was used to having different food options available to him. But when he moved to Louisiana, he was shocked to find that he couldn't eat the way he used to unless he learned to do it himself. He eventually got the hang of it and as he settled in, he spent most of his time focusing on his football career and the new lease on his childhood dream of winning a championship that he had been chasing for years.

Since he'd redshirted his freshman year at Ohio State, Joe was technically considered a redshirt junior during his first year at LSU. He was named the starting quarterback as soon as he transferred and the football practices got rolling. For fans of LSU, however, they weren't sure if Joe was going to be the answer to the issues the team had faced in the past, and those who know the LSU fans know that the quarterbacks are usually the most criticized and talked about players, so there was definitely a lot of pressure on Joe to perform well. Given that he'd been at Ohio State but hadn't played much over the past few years, there were doubts about what he'd be able to do and why he hadn't been given the chance to do anything at Ohio State. Still, the coaches and Joe knew that they had something they could both make work and they were all very eager for the 2018 season to kick off.

His first season at LSU started off well. Against the number seven seeded Auburn early on in the season, Joe showed up and let everyone see some of that untapped potential that had been sitting on the bench at Ohio State for the past few years. He threw for 249 yards in that game and had a touchdown that led to LSU taking the win in the close 22-21 game. The week after that, he was named the SEC Offensive Player of the Week, already making waves in just a few weeks than he'd been able to in his three years at Ohio State. Just a few weeks later, the Tigers were up against his uncle's alma mater, Ole Miss. In this game, Joe again showed up, throwing three touchdowns and a total of 292 yards. He was once again named the SEC Offensive Player of the Week, twice receiving the honor within the opening months of the season.

Throughout the rest of the season, more and more LSU fans and others began to get on board with Joe and what he had to offer. He ended up leading the team to a 10-3 record and even a bowl game. Joe and the Tigers faced off against the University of Central Florida in the Fiesta Bowl. The Tigers ended up taking the win there as well and even launched themselves into a number six ranking in the final AP Poll of the season. Over the course of that first season at LSU, Joe had thrown for 2,894 yards, a number much like the numbers he was putting up in high school. He also had 16 touchdowns for the season and just five interceptions in all thirteen games. Considering the fact that he was now playing almost way more minutes and snaps than ever, it was no surprise that he had a few errors, but he was doing much better. He showed off that dual-threat side of his game by adding another 399 rushing yards as well as a total of seven rushing touchdowns for the season.

Changing schools and taking his football career and future into his own hands was a huge deal and one that could have ended up poorly. However, it was clear after that first year that both Joe, Coach Orgeron, and the rest of the LSU community had found something special within each other and they were excited to see what Joe would have up his sleeve in the following year, his last of eligibility. Everyone was ready to see the young man who had come from practically a nowhere town and had been sitting on the bench as untapped potential come alive in his second season as a starting college quarterback because those who saw him knew that the more snaps he took, the better he was getting and he wasn't done yet.

IT ALL FALLS INTO PLACE

The following year, his senior year, marked another special change for Joe. Although his mother had regularly gone to the LSU games while he was there, his dad hadn't been able to. As the defensive coordinator for the Ohio Bobcats, Jim was always working on the days that his son played and he hadn't been able to go to many games to watch Joe. However, that senior year, Jim decided to retire from his position, ending a 40-year coaching career that span different schools. Jim was ending a chapter in his own book but knew that it would be worth it in order to get to go to Joe's games during his last season as a college quarterback.

At the start of the season, Joe led the team against Georgia Southern. In this game, he was able to throw for an outstanding five touchdowns as he finished the game with 278 passing yards and the team took the victory in the 55-3 landslide opener. Due to his performance in this game, he once more took home an SEC Offensive Player of the Week honor, but this time, he split the title with Tua Tagovailoa, the quarterback out of Alabama. The following week, Joe did even better. As they faced off against number nine, Texas, the Tigers were in for a much more difficult game. Still, Joe was able to throw for four touchdowns and only a single interception. He racked up 471 yards, marking him in the second-place slot for the most yards thrown in a single game for LSU, second only to Rohan Davey who had 528 in 2001 when the Tigers were up against Alabama. The Tigers were able to pull out the win against Texas 45-38 and he received another Player of the Week honor for back-to-back performances.

Not only that, however, he was also named the Walter Camp National Offensive Player of the Week after that game and had really begun to create a buzz around his name and his performance. Now, schools all over were beginning to take a much closer look at the senior quarterback and they weren't the only ones. The NFL teams and sports journalists were hinting at how he might perform at a professional level.

And Joe wasn't done yet. In fact, it seemed like his former Ohio State teammate, Barrett, had been right; all Joe needed was a chance and, here at LSU, he was finally getting it. In Week 3, he threw for another 398 yards. This time, however, he didn't just come second in a school record; he ended up setting a new one by scoring six passing touchdowns that week. Needless to say, with such a great performance from their quarterback and receivers, they easily defeated Vanderbilt 66-38. Again, Joe was named the SEC Offensive Player of the Week afterward. This marked the third time in three weeks that he'd received the honor and really began his senior year with a bang, with his dad there to watch. Additionally, he also marked himself with those performances as the first quarterback in LSU history to have thrown for over 350 yards in three back-to-back games. And then, he did it again the following week with another 344 yards against Utah State. The Tigers took home the easy win 42-6 as Joe threw for five touchdowns in that game as well.

It wasn't until the following week, the fifth week of the season, that his streak came to an end against the number seven seeded Florida. He only managed 293 yards in that game, breaking the 300 plus streak, but he still managed to throw three touchdown passes. LSU took home their next victory that day as well, winning the game 42-28 in a tremendous start to their season. During the following week, Joe was already surpassing the number of single-season passing touchdowns ever thrown by an LSU quarterback. He threw four against Mississippi State that week and moved to a total of 28 touchdowns for the season, marking him as the number one record holder for the school. Then, he continued to perform well and capitalize on the flow of the offense when they faced number nine, Auburn, and he threw 321 yards, setting the record for games over 300 passing yards at LSU. He added two touchdowns to the outcome against Auburn and the Tigers were able to secure yet another win against a top ten rated team that season.

By early November, Joe and the Tigers had done enough to earn them a top-rated position when the rankings were released. They ended up being ranked second, followed by Alabama, their next adversary. The game on November 9th marked a huge occasion for the college football community. Not only were two top three teams facing off against each other, but both teams had something in common beyond their great beginning of the season record: star quarterbacks. Alabama's Tua Tagovailoa, who had shared Co-Offensive Player of the Week honors with Joe early in the year, had been having a great year as well. Not only that, but he, just like Joe, was now being considered in the running for that year's Heisman Trophy award. Needless to say, it was a highly anticipated matchup, and a ton of people tuned in to see how these two teams would perform against each other. And fans, scouts, and rivals were not disappointed. The game ended with a close score of 46-41. Thanks to a solid performance by Joe, the Tigers walked away with the win. Not only did he have 393 passing yards in that game, but he also had three touchdowns with the help of his teammate, Clyde Edwards-Helaire, who he shared the SEC Co-Offensive Player of the Week honors with for their terrific teamwork and performance against Alabama. Additionally, Joe took home another Walter Camp National Offensive Player of the Week honor for the big game.

However, the season wasn't over yet and LSU, now on a roll, was ready to take their game as far as they possibly could, much to the delight of their fans who had been waiting for so long for a quarterback and program like they were seeing this season. The week after the big Alabama game, the Tigers were up against Ole Miss and Joe managed to outdo himself in a number of ways. First, he had a total of 489 passing yards, then he managed five touchdown passes in that game, and finally ended up surpassing Rohan Davey's 2001 record for the most passing yards in a single season. Not only that, he had a streak throughout that game of seventeen completed passes in a row, a new LSU record as well.

By the end of November, the team was looking at the possibility of a completely undefeated regular-season record. However, they had to face Texas A&M before they could secure it. In that game, Joe was in fine form, much like he had been the rest of the season. He threw for three touchdowns and 352 yards, leading the team to the 50-7 win, securing that immaculate record. Over the course of the game, he also managed to set a new record for the SEC as the most single-season passing yards, surpassing the previous record-holder, Kentucky's Tim Couch. As if that wasn't enough, he also tied the SEC record for single-season touchdowns, tying Missouri's Drew Lock and also marked himself as the top spot in SEC single-season touchdowns when he added four more during the SEC Championship game the following week. With those four touchdowns, Joe and the Tigers managed to dominate Georgia in the Championship, taking the win 37-10 and secured a spot in the College Football Playoff. Although their season wasn't over, this marked a milestone for Joe. He had finally gotten the chance to accomplish his childhood dream of winning a championship, and now, with their playoff berth, he could win an even bigger one.

However, before that could happen, something else was brewing for Joe and some of the other stars of the college football league. December marked the Heisman Trophy award and Joe was named the winner. He wasn't just the 2019 Heisman Trophy winner though; he had done it by beating all of the other candidates by the largest margin of victory seen since the award was created, showing that everyone recognized how talented he was and how much potential he had always had and could possibly still have in the future.

With such a momentous award and honor dropped on him, he was truly honored and excited to accept it. While giving his acceptance speech during the ceremony, he not only thanked his team, his coaches, and his family, but he also turned the speech into something more than just a thank you. In his speech on December 14, 2019, Joe shared what it was like to grow up in the small town of Athens and some of the things that he saw happening in his community there. What he wanted people to know about the most was that although people might think of Athens as the place he had come from, it was more than that, and the people there, especially the children, like the ones he'd grown up around, were struggling with poverty and food insecurity. He shared about children going hungry and what it was like to see those kids at school and around town and hoped to shed light on it, bring awareness to it, and hopefully inspire others to help with places like Athens and the kids who lived there and went hungry night after night. His speech ended up moving a lot of people as more than 13,000 people were inspired and ended up donating $450,000 toward the local food banks in Athens County, meaning that so many more kids and families were going to have what they needed for a bit longer and not have to go hungry like they had been.

With such a terrific regular season, capped by a Heisman award, it was truly a season to remember, and one that he got to share with his family as they came to see him play, even his dad. Additionally, Joe was awarded a number of other honors for his performances that season as well. He was awarded the Maxwell Award, Walter Camp Award, Johnny Unitas Golden Arm Award, Davey O'Brien Award, Lombardi Awards, and Manning Award, marking his season as a record-setting one that would go down in history as one of the greatest. He was honored with the awards of the greats who had come before him and he hoped to take that momentum and use it to lead his team in the College Football Playoffs as well.

LSU went into the playoff semifinals facing fourth-seeded Oklahoma in the 2019 Peach Bowl. Here, Joe truly performed well and led under pressure as they secured the win 63-28. Joe had thrown for a terrific 29 for 39 in that game, adding 493 passing yards to his stats and throwing for a total of seven touchdowns, all of which were thrown in the first half of the game. Not only that, but he ended up rushing a bit as well for 22 yards, but it was enough for him to secure an eighth touchdown, this one a rushing one. By scoring a combined eight touchdowns, not only did he lead his team to victory, but he also put himself in the record books by setting a new FBS bowl game record as well as an SEC single-game record. As if that wasn't amazing enough, he had managed all eight touchdowns in just over one half of the game before sitting out the remainder of the game. To this day, people talk about how great of a performance that was and how that game was one of the best ever in college football history.

But Joe and his LSU teammates weren't done just yet. That win launched them into the 2020 National Championship Game. Here, they faced Clemson, a team that had been having a great season as well, and the game was expected to be a good matchup. However, Joe performed really well and blew them away again, albeit not as much as in the game against Oklahoma. Against Clemson, he managed 463 passing yards, which led to five passing touchdowns and he added in a rushing one as well to bring the total up to six. The Tigers defeated Clemson 42-25 and took home the Championship title, making Joe's dream of becoming a Championship college football player a reality. Not only had they gone through the regular season undefeated, but they also took home the Championship and Joe the Heisman.

Over the course of that season, Joe had thrown for 60 touchdowns, which broke the previous record of 58 that had been set by Colt Brennan back in 2006. Additionally, by throwing for 5,671 yards that season,

Joe managed to tie the third-highest in an FBS season, matching Case Keenum's 2009 numbers. Overall, he was given a passer rating of 202 for that year, setting yet another record, with the name Joe Burrow now attached to it. It was clear to everyone that the Tigers and Joe especially had had one heck of a season, but for some, they consider Joe's performance one of the best seasons, if not *the* best, ever to be played by a college quarterback.

Although it had taken him a few years to try his hand at Ohio State only to find himself being passed over, Joe hadn't given up. By putting his nose to the grindstone for his early degree, he was able to set things up nicely for him to transfer and be able to play two years at a school that would give him a chance. When he was leaving high school, he had thought he'd be winning championships at Ohio State, his hometown state, but in the end, leaving ended up being the best thing that he could have done. Not only did he prove that he was capable, talented, and had a lot of untapped potentials, LSU gave him a community that rallied behind him, believed in him, and placed their faith in him, and he did not let them down. Now, LSU fans can look back on Joe's time there and remember the stellar season that he gave them during his final season. And now that he'd had the chance to prove himself, he'd won a national championship like he'd dreamed. And now that he is done with his college eligibility, Joe was ready to tackle the next level of play: the NFL.

MOVING TO THE BIG LEAGUES

Making the transition from the college level to the professional one may seem like a natural next step for many star athletes. However, although they may perform well in college, year after year, stars at their own schools or conferences end up drafted and put on an NFL roster, only to get washed out in the first year or find themselves relegated to the bench for much of their career. Still, as Joe was making his way through the transition, having a national championship title and being a Heisman winner had to count for a lot, and as soon as he got close to ending his college career, commentators, journalists, and teams in the NFL were all interested in what Joe would be up to in the following season. Needless to say, Joe's name would be making the rounds as the NFL draft talk commenced.

Leading up to the event, many were speculating about his game and deeply analyzing his pros and cons. Although he had had a good run as a junior at LSU, it wasn't really until his senior year that he was able to turn tons of heads. In fact, by some accounts, he started his senior year, after a so-so junior year, a 200 to 1 shot at the Heisman, but halfway through that senior season, he managed to create enough buzz and produce enough great numbers that he had become the favorite to win it, which he did. Still, with just one tremendous year before launching into the pros, it was no wonder that many people and scouts were curious as to what he would be like when he advanced to the next level.

In many reports from scouting agencies, he had a lot of great attributes that they saw and were excited about. Everything from his poise to his ability to read the defense were discussed with tons of praise. In fact, based on many of those reports, the number one positive that Joe had going for him wasn't his speed or even his accuracy or strength; it was his intelligence. Not only was he great at reading the defense and anticipating how the play would unfold, but what he lacked in other aspects, he was able to make up in his decision-making in split-second moments.

That sort of ability is one that is hard to teach or learn. By the time you get to the peak of the college level, you have to have a certain amount of football IQ and intelligence in order to make it there. But in the NFL, you'd be facing off against veterans who had seemingly seen it all and done it all a hundred times. Still, the outlook for Joe's ability to use his mind to take advantage of every situation he could out there on the field was great. Teams, especially those that needed a quarterback now, and not in a few years, were anxiously hoping to get a shot at that brain and that quick thinking.

As far as downsides go, although he was a talented athlete and had been for many years, he wasn't at the top of his game as a quarterback. With others in the NFL like Tom Brady, Aaron Rodgers, and Drew

Brees, Joe's throwing arm didn't seem as powerful and sometimes not as accurate, even at the college level. He had a good placement, and many times it was due to his quick thinking and decision-making that he could make those throws, but it still left a bit to be desired. However, one of the best things about having that sort of flaw, according to scouts, is that it can be worked on. It can be taught and coached, something that many NFL teams were willing to invest in to get the rest of the Joe Burrow package.

Despite those flaws, it was clear to everyone that Joe was destined for a high pick; after all, he was the Heisman winner last year and had put up tremendous numbers. Unfortunately, due to the COVID-19 pandemic, things happened a bit differently for the 2020 draft process. Still, he was able to do many video interviews with teams in the NFL even though there was no combine or workouts with them. He talked to many teams, many, in fact, that didn't have a top-five berth in the draft. This, he said, led to some interesting conversations as teams that were out of the top five would tell him that they knew they had no shot at drafting him, so they instead chatted with him about life and the excitement of moving into the NFL instead of really considering him for their team.

Due to the quarantine rules in place in many places, even in Las Vegas where the draft was supposed to be held, Joe now found himself sitting at his parents' home in Athens, Ohio on the night of the draft instead of dressing up and getting ready to make his way across the stage. When asked about his plans for the draft ahead of time, he said he just planned to watch it on TV sitting on his parents' couch with his family around him, far from the more glamorous and exciting event that usually took place. Still, he said, he wasn't too disappointed because it meant that he could share the moment with his family around him, and that meant a lot to him.

In this draft, Joe and 57 other top college players were invited to be interviewed as part of the virtual draft. Leading up to this, there was a lot of speculation about Joe and his comparison to Alabama's Tua Tagovailoa, who he had faced off against at LSU and come out the victor. Joe understood that they were the top quarterback prospects and many projected Joe to go first, followed by Tua. As the draft commenced, Joe and his family around him sat back and waited to see what was going to happen and whether the claims from sportscasters were correct.

The Cincinnati Bengals opened the draft with the first pick. And when they announced who they wanted, it was not a surprise to most when the commissioner said Joe's name. When asked about the possibility of being the first-round pick ahead of time, Joe was excited about the chance to play for Cincinnati.

As an Ohio boy, Joe had grown up and spent most of his time rooting for the local colleges and he eventually found himself at Ohio State when it came time for him to go to college as well. However, when he transferred, it was bittersweet due to the fact that he was leaving his home state's team without having won a championship for them and did it for LSU instead. He said that many people were asking him about playing for Cincinnati because it was a chance for him to come home again and play for an Ohio team just like he'd hoped as a kid. Well, with the first-round pick, it looked like he was going to get that and so were the Ohioans.

As the first overall pick, Joe marked the third straight year that a Heisman winning quarterback was selected as the first pick overall. He followed behind Baker Mayfield and Kyler Murray in the previous drafts. As he prepared to make his move back to Ohio a more permanent thing, he signed his four-year rookie contract with the Bengals for $36.1 million at the end of July. Although he'd been stuck in his parents' home during the quarantine, it now looked like he'd be closer to home for a while playing for the Bengals, something that worked well for all parties involved. Everyone was excited to see what he'd do for the Bengals and how well he would translate to the NFL. In fact, before the season even began, he was projected to be the NFL Offensive Rookie of the Year, putting some weight on his shoulders, which he was happy to carry.

OFF THE FIELD

Even before signing his contract with the Bengals, Joe was already getting offered other contracts. In fact, just a few days before the draft, his name was trending as a result of the tweets put out by Lowe's. He ended up signing a few other endorsement deals as well, making him a quick $700,000 before he'd even played in his first professional game. He made endorsement deals with not only Lowe's but also Bose, Nerf, and Buffalo Wild Wings. As a result, he declared, after signing with the Bengals for that huge rookie contract, that he'd use his endorsement money instead. He planned to put his contract money aside and save it all while he lived off the $700,000 instead, something that many agree is right in line with his intelligence on the field and his ability to look ahead at the future.

With his Heisman speech, Joe managed to bring not only attention but money and resources back into his community. He helped local food banks and provided awareness about childhood hunger and poverty that are prevalent in many of the small towns like Athens. Obviously, he has a heart that reaches out, even when he is being honored. In addition, many of the local Ohioans became LSU fans, donning their purple shirts in support of Joe even if they had to shun some of the more local teams. Both of these facts show just how influential and inspiring Joe has been to many people. In fact, there are those in his own family who have looked to Joe as inspiration as well.

Joe's older brother, Jamie, and Jamie's wife, Codie, relied heavily on Joe's final season at LSU as a way to cope through the difficult time they were going through. Although the couple had a son, Jamie IV, they found out that their dream of having three children together would be coming true with the addition of twins that Codie was carrying. Their dream had been to have two boys and a girl, and with a boy and girl twin on the way, they got exactly what they had hoped for. Everyone in the family was excited and the couple had already decorated their nursery Toby by the time Codie was four months pregnant, some things in blue and others in pink.

However, on March 20, 2019, Jamie received a call that his wife's water had broken, several months too soon. He drove immediately back to his home in Nebraska from Iowa where he had been on a business trip. Just two days later, the couple lost the twins, they had had a miscarriage. This was such a devastating moment for the family, not just Jamie and Codie, but for all of the Burrow crew. They had all been anxious to see the twins come into this world and it was difficult for them to deal with the heartbreak of losing them. Codie and Jamie spent time grieving and learning to lean on their family as support.

One thing, however, helped them when they were ready to get back to the day-to-day world as they continued to grieve: Joe's games. That senior season, Joe had so many tremendous games, and oftentimes, his family was there to support him or were watching at home. Jamie shared later that the miscarriage had been incredibly difficult for them and that he still had trouble speaking about it six months after the fact. However, he said that one thing that helped was Joe's outstanding season. Watching Joe play in his final year at LSU brought the family joy and while he was out there doing his thing, it made it easier for Jamie and Codie to turn their minds away from the grief for a few hours and support their younger brother. It provided them the time they needed to process their loss and helped them to find the support they needed to get through the pain.

As many people tuned in on Saturdays and saw Joe warming up, his parents in the Tiger tent with a sign that said "Burrow gang," it was probably the last thing anyone could imagine given the recent tragedy the family had witnessed. However, their closeness and Joe's games helped them all to get much closer to each other.

No matter what happens in Joe's NFL career in the future, there are a few things he's accomplished that nobody can take away from him. For one, his ability to go from benchwarmer to Heisman winner is something that will likely end up being a great movie one day. Nobody could have pegged him as that type of turnaround story, but he did it anyway. He left his mark at LSU by breaking various records and brought a splash of purple to his Ohio fans. Additionally, his senior season was one that shocked and awed the football community regarding how clean and great it was. Truly, Joe's name will go down in history, and he has only just begun his professional career.

MORE FROM JACKSON CARTER BIOGRAPHIES

My goal is to spark the love of reading in young adults around the world. Too often children grow up thinking they hate reading because they are forced to read material they don't care about. To counter this we offer accessible, easy to read biographies about sportspeople that will give young adults the chance to fall in love with reading.

Go to the Website Below to Join Our Community

https://mailchi.mp/7cced1339ff6/jcbcommunity

Or Find Us on Facebook at

www.facebook.com/JacksonCarterBiographies

As a Member of Our Community You Will Receive:

First Notice of Newly Published Titles

Exclusive Discounts and Offers

Influence on the Next Book Topics

Don't miss out, join today and help spread the love of reading around the world!

OTHER WORKS BY JACKSON CARTER BIOGRAPHIES

Patrick Mahomes: The Amazing Story of How Patrick Mahomes Became the MVP of the NFL

Donovan Mitchell: How Donovan Mitchell Became a Star for the Salt Lake City Jazz

Luka Doncic: The Complete Story of How Luka Doncic Became the NBA's Newest Star

The Eagle: Khabib Nurmagomedov: How Khabib Became the Top MMA Fighter and Dominated the UFC

Lamar Jackson: The Inspirational Story of How One Quarterback Redefined the Position and Became the Most Explosive Player in the NFL

Jimmy Garoppolo: The Amazing Story of How One Quarterback Climbed the Ranks to Be One of the Top Quarterbacks in the NFL

Zion Williamson: The Inspirational Story of How Zion Williamson Became the NBA's First Draft Pick

Kyler Murray: The Inspirational Story of How Kyler Murray Became the NFL's First Draft Pick

Do Your Job: The Leadership Principles that Bill Belichick and the New England Patriots Have Used to Become the Best Dynasty in the NFL

Turn Your Gaming Into a Career Through Twitch and Other Streaming Sites: How to Start, Develop and Sustain an Online Streaming Business that Makes Money

From Beginner to Pro: How to Become a Notary Public

Made in the USA
Monee, IL
08 December 2022

20120517R00026